# POTENTIAL STRANGER

PHOENIX POETS

# Potential Stranger

KILLARNEY CLARY

THE UNIVERSITY OF CHICAGO PRESS
*Chicago and London*

KILLARNEY CLARY was born in Los Angeles in 1953. She has two books of poems, *Who Whispered Near Me* and *By Common Salt*.

The University of Chicago Press, Chicago 60637
The University of Chicago Press, Ltd., London

Printed in the United States of America

12 11 10 09 08 07 06 05 04 03 1 2 3 4 5

ISBN: 0-226-10930-5 (cloth)
ISBN: 0-226-10931-3 (paper)

Library of Congress Cataloging-in-Publication Data

Clary, Killarney.
Potential Stranger / Killarney Clary.
p. cm.—(Pheonix poets)
ISBN 0-226-10930-5 (cloth : alk. paper)
ISBN 0-226-10931-3 (paper : alk. paper)
I. Title. II. Series.

PS3553 .L345 P68 2003
811′.54—dc21

2002067331

♾ The paper used in this publication meets the minimum requirements of the American National Standard for Information Sciences—Permanence of Paper for Printed Library Materials, ANSI Z39.48-1992.

*for my father*

*Clark had written, 'Ocian in view! O! the joy!' He was mistaken. Tonight's camp is near Pillar Rock and the ocean cannot be seen from there.*

— BERNARD DE VOTO, *The Journals of Lewis and Clark*

# *Contents*

# *Acknowledgments*

Grateful acknowledgment is made to the periodicals in which these poems first appeared:

*American Poetry Review*: "El Paso," "The boy had told a rhyme," "The last sure thing"
*Antioch Review*: "To tell you"
*Black Warrior Review*: "I tested my cream kid slippers"
*Colorado Review*: "I dove to where there was no light," "Two magpies"
*Conduit*: "All that isn't me," "Elm leaf shadows"
*Faultline*: "A clear membrane," "The lip of a yellow snapdragon," "A bitter front arrives"
*Indiana Review*: "Two notes," "The body says it can put forth," "His body is a pendulum," "My love of the surprise," "One, gentled"
*jubilat*: "Toward you where you must be," "Would I dive"
*LIT*: "Beneath pageantry," "The widening sidewalk"
*Ploughshares*: "Confetti lifts over the fairground"
*Poetry Review*: "At junctures"
*Portland Review:* "Any one of us," "A small stranger," "It's hot"
*The Recorder*: "Pieces that jammed," "You come as smoke"
*Seneca Review*: "The exchange rat"
*Salon.com*: "Two notes"
*Solo*: "Above San Xavier"

"In this wind" appeared in *The Geography of Home: California's Poetry of Place,* edited by Christopher Buckley and Gary Young (Heyday Books, 1999).

I would like to thank the Lannan Foundation for their continued encouragement and for a residency in Marfa, Texas, and the Wurlitzer Foundation for a residency in Taos, New Mexico.

# POTENTIAL STRANGER

Toward you where you must be, between God and my doll, I send a secret—my frayed hem. But you might answer.

I touch her plastic lips. I take her stiff hand missing its little finger, push it to my thumb. I tell Him, "Whatever you want."

But to you I send a postcard. "I'd like to see you, too."

The log records preparations—preserved meat, allotments of water to weigh against delays caused by weather, equipment failure. Great industry cleans the heart blank so it will be ready. Where will the first drop of vibrant disappointment fall in the clear dish?

Each born slightly misshapen, these banded men prepare for their performance, entirely skilled to play against the golden mean. As if everyday deformity helps plates spin on their poles or high wire to thicken. As if the dark jewel of spirit can be disguised with silver lipstick or a pointed head. They come out of the rain; between the wheels of the caravan they try an easy game together. But he had smiled and talked to her. They had danced. After that autumn season she heard of his shows—new acts and standards, his first nearly fatal fall. He didn't ask her again.

One, gentled against his nature, stills for the flaming hoop. Another tenses at the sound of flapping canvas, and there's talk of a quick show.

I smell what evaporates, taste what dissolves. You aren't carrying the feather boa I expected, but a string of iridescent pigeons. I greet you as you leave, a spark trailing after you like a foul prank. A fool whistles in the dressing tent. Roustabouts mutter, spit bad luck into the dry grass.

The big cat jumps fine, but the radio plays tornado static. This country is so flat I see the curve in the horizon, a prairie fire on the rim. We'd better tie down, or run.

At junctures we renamed the roads for what happened there: Glasses Lost, Insult, Why Are There No Ghosts. We never returned to the places, and though our trackers felt they learned our history, the sequence was senseless. We could have faced nearly any direction, since what drove us was a desire to occur without erasing what we'd made.

We agreed. We were not scared; we wouldn't be caught. No children. We held hands in ceremony but were uneasy with it. We each had our own pack. We didn't even envy birds.

The man has lost his way in the snow and he prays, lies against a stone as he grows sleepier. In the shape of the branches above, what does he see that assures him? The light is weak; the edges of the picture dull.

What will be found when the snow melts? When the reservoir is drained? That quick shadow below the bridge has something pressing to tell about nearly effortless transformation.

I want to complete a deliberate action, make a single perfect offering. What will be left? I was once on both sides of a patch of sunlight on a baby's arm. Not mere memory, but attar.

The body says it can put forth. Salt. Maps rising onto skin.

The place sought so often wears raw and colorless from pointers so that the crossroads isn't clear. Bareness tells me about treasure.

As I fold the grass back from the mark, brush loose topsoil, the routes repel.

How dare I?

Icy air presses on the tableland, a sheet of urgency. Plans hiss through dry courses. They grab at dogged raggedness but it tears away.

Frayed ribbons whip against themselves in the rising wind. They had been a celebration. Those who tried to hold them call for salve and forgetting.

The mountain takes its privacy; night laughs again. I swallow one morsel and tighten on its travel.

We climbed to a high altitude. Dull from it, I rested in his presence. The wander of my dreams and limbs drew fast under a heavy sky. He waited while I slept, and where we'd ridden a few hours before, the snow started down, straight and strange as too early a trust, adding to itself with held breath. I woke and fell again from a pale tether: the rattle of his thumbnail across ribs of corduroy.

Bright planet, dressed in a veil of violet tulle, gold light from many windows, do I wish otherwise?

When the fine strands freeze and split, and bits of purple scatter then gather in the creases, the grid fractures, adjustments are made without reference—fluid in a bottle of liquid glass. For a moment.

Then you remain behind gestures and posture, inside what is said and the manner of birth. I remake the invitation: if my expression must always be your costume, please, lead the dance that keeps threads tense but unbroken.

A bitter front arrives and I lie my face against its cold white placket, one button rough at my temple. There is solace here in the enclosure of darkening snow. Scraps of heat race to rescue elixir until it is the last bit, protected inside the ferment of the barest touch of a strong hand on my nape, smell of beeswax. Here I am, in the arms of the end, and here is the world I loved for its fretting, pushing me away.

Pieces that jammed when forced, tore when pulled apart. Grit fell under fireworks and stars leaked through the smudge. Bonfires leveed the procession of the palette upon which the statue danced. Body of pieces.

The dark crowd shifted and whirred. I put my hand on the stranger's back because we walked on ice—no surprise at my touch. Body of falling snow, of cinders, falling. Body of ashes. A dead man's reading glasses on a drain grate. A limp mantilla at the back of a drawer. What proof of an afterlife do we need? A vision burned into an old shirt.

Early on the day of the reception I lit new candles and extinguished them. The wicks were charred, the wax untouched. Ready.

Two magpies in the field seem to mark my time. The map is a brand—I own this life, or the record of how it was spilled.

Then, at empty, the body provides. At sacrifice of purpose, my fingertips take in food from the steamy scalp, or of stray grains that nestle in the whorls. I can't set this by; I grow heavy on a fare of fume.

Where one lands, where the catch is buried, the itinerary of scrub or rut—is measure. The grass reddens in the day's finish. What is nourished pushes beyond compass, sharpens to silhouette in the desert freeze.

All that isn't me is here too, shifting when I move, guiding me with weather and intelligence, a hand on my left shoulder as I walk between downed power lines, through the dark town where even transistor radios have gone silent. A stranger laughs, so I am tired.

Ochre leaves quivered across bright lenses, caught in the tangled reflection on a butter knife that flashed in a mirror, off the mirror to the cement floor.

A bubble of mercury wobbled in the switch. You came toward me on the sidewalk and as we passed I might have fallen into you or leaned away. Either would have tipped the silver to its end.

Crows galloped, goofy, on the flat, tar roof. I was tapping in a waiting room when the insistent signage overcame me. The limited ways in are worn by rehearsal. When's the show?

I tested my cream kid slippers, pinch of elastic over high insteps, the tackiness of my palms. My timing was on and the ropes pulled evenly. I counted; the music counted. I let go.

Warm air rises wildly. I smell corn oil and burnt sugar. I begin to think the sequence again, but there is no melody this time, there is no touch.

As I drop I remember my body, the anticipation of your wrists in my grip, then, my graceless flapping. The explanations, the want of them, vanish. "I know you meant to be there"—vanishes.

I exhale the live moment before the applause, before even guesswork that figures the trick sparks in each bright, jammed head.

To tell you. I was trying to concentrate. I watched you; everyone in the tent watched you. I would be hero, called for at the moment of my preparedness, but, thinking, I was pulled away from my weight.

The background swelled. Electric children, the way they hunger for a slip-up; in the north ring, white horses, their cumbersome ballet; a fight in the blue seats—I was taken. Great communal inhale. Then. If that silence could have been my disappearance . . .

Muffled through the side walls, the Opener for the Congress of Freaks beckons the curious come witness simple differences stretched and squeezed to amaze the innocent. Your back is arched over the ringbank until the rubbery buffoons lift you and dance, wobbling their limp limbs with your limp limbs while the arc of the fly bar dwindles.

A truck pulled up. Footsteps on the gravel drive lagged at the windows. Two men in jeans and white T-shirts stooped at the faucet, talked a little; one fingered the dry threads. They worked surely, laughed as they stood, watered tufts of grass in the sandy soil.

With standard prayers thick in your bones, a dependable simplicity fortified, you answer me with what you want—a smile, Sunday afternoon.

Dishes I break and I watch them break. My project requires disorder, the sanctuary of replacing pieces. You cannot help me fix this. Erratic amen.

We bent for potsherds, silver, money cowries at the tide line, and the hope of something never seen before, for which we'd find use. Trapped once in a box canyon of cholla and ocotillo at dusk, their spines aglow, cool air sinking between us, I found a curl of black bone, pocketed it before you looked. Other discoveries we celebrated—your trout, the last sunlight in the redwoods. I wanted you to win. I didn't mean to keep count.

No one promised to go with me to Texas or the market, into the next hour here in Los Angeles where I've set the house plants on the porch so they won't be bored or suspect that the anxiety of stillness sucks up all options. As if they want. I had an idea that there is certainty, an object maybe, stone in my hand or sun on my face, but there's not a thing I would call real. No one coming with me toward the mountains, the streams of the forks of the San Gabriel River, on the crunch of dry brash on the creature earth that lets me ride. All dream. Not even the itch or cut or blood from the cut or cold water on it, trout in a shadow, camouflage of reflection, or the leaves that fall to meet their pictures. Again I meet my picture and will not promise myself what lies there. Light off the moon as if there were a moon.

If I could gather silence into myself—a lighthouse.

Here I am; stay clear.

Barely light, still an arc of shine trembles to one side of the raindrop in a crease in your toughened forearm. With tilt or mass it reshapes, runs off. You watch this, the many miles you've traveled humming in your frame. Rain without pause for eleven days. No dry shirt or blanket, tents rotted, specimens tainted, and not a minute of silence between the unseen ocean and the rising river, until foresight is without outline in your head. You rub oil onto metal, condensing your regret, recording that you have missed your appointment with discovery.

His body is a pendulum, the bob of it. The knot of his arms in leather cord masters a nearly silent flight while his bare, ordinary toes whisper a circle on the polished stage. His muscles are made gruesome by dusty white tights. Best I don't recognize the smell or gulp down too soon. He appears to do nothing, leaden in harness; and in the tick when spectators cough, shift in the stands or touch their straws to open lips, the plea that holds between his finale and presence is absolute while he revolves around his shadow, until heat is dislodged, and my reach, atomized.

The last sure thing that night was my patent leather shoe. Darkness lifted me in his warm shirt and cold jacket. Old voices. Lighted wheel rolling on the lake. The pulse of my day lost its measure; I could feel endlessness and belong there. The lights fell and touched themselves and rose up—by motions repeated, taken and complete.

He tied his ankle to mine and we hobbled from the lunchroom toward the ribbon. If we'd agreed on how to start we might have won. Coarse grass, patched. Tiny salmon-colored flowers in the weeds. We didn't talk, didn't place, turned to our separate friends, and I worried ahead to relays, drifted or counted, rubbed the sore bone under my white sock. No person was cruel, only a yawning which recitations couldn't fill. After seven hours each day for nine years we dumped our books into satchels, our surnames printed in black block on the paper covers, rode home with our ballast of silent effect.

Confetti lifts over the fairground. Happy music, played to make us happy, slows its parade, dims as it pivots at the curb. While I hide in the copse, the outlines lighten, my skeleton, luminescent. I take the thick cup in both hands, drink urgently. Warm wind plays litter across the yard.

My company's shattered glass, a shallow receding puddle where a goldfish puffs away, where chips of eggshell shiver on the surface, color bleeds from tissue, and the sky tries to settle. I win if I'm found by the day's end.

Leaves clatter on the breezeway, tapping blind, shoaling, begging me, my frame as it locks to itself, as I swallow—to rise.

Into the land of youth, westward, to the place of starting again, cities of gold, on the coast of promise—mysterious cure—a mirror's thrown down, and so without luck, without reflection we stop.

We have come to the beginning, the finish of the country, itinerary worn out, facing the surf—what sailors smell as land. We ask detailed questions. None of us can tell, so we tug on each other, "Come. Look."

In this lull, one at the tide line stoops to pick at foam and weeds; another builds a fire. The intended didn't arrive and there is no new plan. As the sun lowers, we face the mountains, consider what we have passed, and fall to dreaming, to scrounging.

I dove to where there was no light, among huge pale tethered worms, and waved about as if nothing mattered. Their congregation kept my track, knew more than I about my passage. Hard to believe anything could live so cold and deep, but we are explorers. This or its like, had to be, here, or soon.

Who prayed for us, who set yourselves adrift, peregrini in your oarless coracles, or who whipped yourselves in adobe moradas, for our sake, I hand over to you the worn parcel of woe—purpose.

You, who drop treasures and traps along the road, did I go seeking so resolutely that search changed my direction? Did you keep the folded note of want in your pocket, in your hand in your pocket, in damp fingers that rub ceaselessly—to touch it, to risk erasing it, to stay with us?

Two notes. I wait for a third. If it doesn't come . . . if you don't come to weight me, then what is my shape; where is the space I hold?

You don't come. No blow tenderizes my heart. My wrist turned in the dance is too light, unattached, a thing I knew better last week. Two notes in a standoff, the same in their stubbornness.

With a trace for tare, I would be filled, heavy. Saturate me as I am sinking, spinning in a thick eddy, draining, in search of the tonic. I wouldn't be alone.

When you are the scrub jay, taillights in the fog, when I am compelled to find you everywhere, you still haven't arrived. I'm teased by the cloudy fire opal, a future in water drops beaded on a bare branch, shuddering free. They tell me there's warmth in these clothes, that I was born from you, that you are gone.

You come as smoke, reverence threaded through milky fingers, as a slice of cold light across the fields.

In white noise you dress, your passage a hum below hearing, your taste the taste of teeth.

On the wound's edges, reaching, in the restless lip of candle shadow, you almost fail.

In this wind, the sharp blue cut of the San Gabriels flattens against the neon east; eucalyptus want to break loose but hold, thrashing, to what is. Just air, all air, all tossed and secured at once; and when I see I am in a dry room, listen to the flyer as it's banded to the outer doorknob, I say, "here." But I am all pull.

I am walking in the arroyo. I am in love; I am scared. Everyone is still alive. The leaves aren't sad and restless; the canyon isn't cooling so fast, darkening between its walls as the days shorten and the way narrows. I am not going back. There is no body made to take me back into itself.

Always in the in-between, at ease with my tongue in its pool, or taking a shocking first breath in the bright room in the hands of an expert. Lucky, in-between, where friction finds me.

Wimple and guimpe, sixteen cloth-covered buttons. Fifty-nine jet beads against porcelain. "How can we help you, sweetie, if you won't tell us what's wrong?" Class waiting beyond. Painted games on the blacktop playground beyond. Hedges, honeysuckle, ride home, the wide world. "Tell us why you did it." Pounds per inch. Crumple.

Beneath pageantry, the reason I was elected to crown the statue on her flowered bier with the limp halo of jasmine and baby's breath. Inside ceremony, a tongue's constant temperature.

Dependable liquid structures held each firm and upright in a rank of pairs. Words repeated in unison: "Spotless Mother." What we learned lined up faithfully under fragrant trees despite the exuberance of store-bought lilies, separate from wondering, *Why did they choose me?*

I stood embarrassed, made-up, wearing white cotton gloves and formal uniform. Each offering drew wild at heart, its perfume suspended in damp May morning air, was schooled-in to look ordinary wrapped in wet paper and grips of foil, despite the benediction, hallowed ground, the unfolding. Within public reverence, infection waxed from the center of a white camellia.

Elm leaf shadows fuzz and throb on the flowered paper, scatter in a dry wind. Soul, a moist creature, pulls in and waits, worm pale.

Chlorine and ashes. Pads of the jade plant wither. Lizard on a stone. Limits to this room, to each frame. Red threads of loss weave in private a tighter, reworked stitch of no.

The boy had told a rhyme as he unfastened his pants. He was scolded, ended up in the cab of a big rig with this man he slightly knew, under a clear sky on the straight desert interstate.

On the dock the driver and receiver agreed on the sky's shift, a cold front. Both were in shirt sleeves, laughing. Now the driver went back to the icy waiting room to fetch the boy. On the green vinyl chair he was propped, blood clotting at his mouth; he was shivering. The driver picked him up like an armful of tissue paper. I felt that. I felt his young feathery breath. "My poor boy," I moaned. I was lifted. I was light as a dried leaf, dried brittle star, headlights through falling snow. I was high above the road, traveling.

This is where I am, where I've been before, waiting on the wall with loose papers, my untidy ways, in the scuffle of bare legs and hard shoes, in the want want want of bearing.

Grass where it forces through cracks, dares me. Crows above the playground toss their loud smarts. A true word won't be spoken in my carpool.

The puzzle multiplies and narrows. What honor or disgrace is this ink tattoo the new boy drew in my palm? If I look any closer any longer, if I eat more, call and call, joy swells to a dangerous volume. Nothing simple, or other than itself.

My love of the surprise moving where the rock had been—that was *my* damp, my skin in sleeves, the sock drooping at my heel.

My love, my squirreled treasure, what made me lonely.

I didn't tell about the lidded jar of a hundred snails behind the vaporizer in the bathroom cupboard. I'd collect heart, gather struggle, leave the dead to change color, rubbery and blackening or blasted pale as ice on a salted, bright flat.

An expanse grand to explosion. No skin, homogenous temperature . . . what was, before creation.

Once we could be seen, we had no being.

A microscope dives into a print-smudge resembling the milky way.

Heaven, again.

To have tried to meet, to have swerved at the last, to say we will try again.

Bees of light ricochet in cherry trees against the fast western sky. Seeds in fuzzy explosion lift and swirl, busy before dusk. A neighbor's radio drones news; no one word clear. Semi on the highway. Thunder. Hurry.

Whitecaps, the curve of a spent wake and gray-violet of deep water are the business of the lake. But close to me, Yellow Bay is patient as the soul of a place. It has its own private traffic of ospreys and shadow, shore of warm stones.

It would come in without trouble. I would ease into it, swallow and be swallowed. I only need to cross the pale grass and remove my clothes.

In holding still, want is the food without finish, and I shiver in its abundance.

The lip of a yellow snapdragon wavers before the field. A bee rubs its face in the window on the east side of the cabin. The day travels over me where the sun slants in. A breeze comes up in the evening; cloud-skirts drag across the lake; silver spatters on the rail in twilight.

Frail substance like a flock of small birds, squeezes dark, turns, vanishes, bunches visible again. Slippery life, with all its strings moving, just there, no, there. The hopper travels disguised as a butterfly even after dark.

A clear membrane over stone curls back to lick itself and is shoved on; I follow a spit of foam as it's tossed through clattering shine. The aqua flow, opaque with glacial flour, turns here to ease. The surface quiets and on it fine lines of wind and disturbance play into shapes of countries I don't recognize; leaves travel with their shadows. Maybe tomorrow I will. . . .

Yesterday while tying my shoes I felt an old September tidy and hot. I knew the memory was untrue, but the clean of bright new laces in my fingers and the shoe pulling snug on my foot, heat rising from asphalt to my skin were certain. What do I ever see? The picture now of Swan River removes itself as I gather; blue becomes an emptiness. I lower my face to the water and it is cold.

Flies bump against the front window, each the size of the dull skiff pinned distant on the silver plate of the lake in Sunday heat. Wanting hour. When the night bugs gather outside the glass, I'll be afraid to look at the stars because of the darkness. I'm afraid to go swimming with my neighbor and his friend. I know they wouldn't laugh at my skinny frame or let me drown or make me swim if the water's too cold, but I'm relieved as the day is lost. So when he asks I say no thank you, and look at my watch. Shame. Shame on me for my shame. Translucent wings, red-orange bodies, and the floppy moths. They want to come in. I wonder if they see each other, or do they claim their tracks by touch.

This must be held secret in order for it to be true.

Love. Someone from whom to hide.

The exchange rat brings her offering, maybe borrowed from my own pantry.

I mailed the letter with an aside to fate, “If this contains an insincere word, send it astray.” Now I believe the letter is lost.

I lay a twig on the polished floor, a decent item for trade. I fuss with how it sits, betray I know it doesn’t seem like much, but you might find in the placement and dusting a gift of deliberation.

“Here,” I say as I open my pearl-filled fist for you after you leave.

What is worthy? If you tell me that I love you, if you feel what you receive suffices, yes then.

The magician tugs one luminous corner of carmine silk then yards of triangles, varicolored, tied. A delicate snag at the end, the last tip breaks free and he stands plain in black and white his gloves still, shy foreigners.

Tremble that wails inside the habit of restraint, shudder, secret and alive, thank God I'm scared. For what ever rises, its opposite rises. Not quite seen or heard the bits are precious. Yes, I'm losing. Yes, there is too much.

Shadows give up edge under cloud cover, calming; but nothing ever disappears. The large hands waving horizontally over the hat pretend to work their wonders there in the spot, while in the public dark the irritable woman lays her cool fingers tenderly across her husband's wrist.

Any one of us might have turned away, even so close, held the call tense and echoing against cliffs or skin, because there is a place for our sounds, from which they return. But we couldn't stand or see; we breathed in each other's hair. No matter what we expected, we had to come here, with the river's freedom.

Given your hesitant, determined hands . . .

Once the taste of ocean in the air, and winter inevitable . . .

When reached, ceremony complete, buttons fastened and assumptions broken, desire, tipped by stopping, figured its new map of because.

El Paso. Eleventh floor of the hotel in a dust storm with eight hundred miles of Interstate Ten vibrating behind my eyes. Two nights ago there were two of us. East of Redlands, I was away, and couldn't remember or predict. There spun the windmill blades defiantly, making use.

I hear grains of grit tick against the glass and a howl that won't let up. No time to inhale. On point, I might fall cynical, fall sentimental; they are the same. I want you to stand in front of me and be other. The wall of umber air thins for a span and the city sharpens. I figure as I watch the depot sign dim and clear without pattern the number of interruptions, the shortest distance.

The wind is a knife, knife is this pause, tension in glass. So I've dropped the glass in the sink now and broken it. Windows bow in; eucalyptus are furious as my expectations.

I can pretend my bones shameless. I can run my fingers over my teeth and think, me me me, but I am unconvinced. Even this shelter of skin as I fold into myself against the pointed blast of cold through the hinges is not quite.

Tumbleweeds catch and skip; the fragile clear out. The wind buffets birds into chain link, screams all night and tears across the ridge at dawn. I wait for what will last in me, in the world, find myself laughing as the storm keeps on.

Above San Xavier, scapulars click against wrought iron. A baseball cap with a man's photograph and dates—his wife brought this lament, tied it with a scrap of cloth to the grotto gates where plastic flowers, rosaries, clipped dollars rattle and slap, and the wind doesn't ever stop.

Colored glitter whirls in a dust devil, presses into the mortared rocks, into the folds of the statue's plaster gown. Not a moment's rest for it, for those who pray. For the souls of the departed not a second in which they aren't called upon. *Tell us. Forgive us.* Air pressed through a narrow place whistles a promised rending, marks another durable want.

A bottle thrown from a slowed pick-up shattered on cinder block; the radio bass fooled with my heart. Train engines warned one long blast, clacked over the four town crossings then drew onto the empty plateau. Container cars they pulled were stacked double, enough of them to make an island of these few houses, and they too beat a rhythm, with the wind against their sides then through their couplings. The gates would lift any minute. In the darkness across the street under bat-laden eaves two pale figures flailed silently a signal, not for me.

A small stranger without edges I need this container of *please.* I turn, walk onto Ocotillo Mesa. Their squirrelly arms reach up, tips aflame, a begging frenzy of thorns in a silent hundred degrees.

Offered endless fire they send up their own in return. Some sweet taste rises to meet sugar, and the best answer is a cast of the question. No one knows where I am.

My hands, pressed on your chest, don't go through. There is an other to break against, expectation glittering like a thousand polyhedrons of tempered glass useless now. My palms fill with light.

It's hot and I hear the freeways through all the screened windows wide open. A bright, sharp, half-moon above Echo Park.

One of those perfections. My absolute body, bare limbs moving, a stranger of some interest, a simple, live object.

If any of us saw any of us this way, there could be no misunderstanding.

Love me for my bones which will last awhile.

In ratio, in a progression which lured us into separate lands, due to pleasing proportion, the prize was won and held. The reward is this: each is where it was ordained to be. The logic of law should release me, but I want to walk straight into the Pacific breakers at high tide toward where the sun splays. Like that.

Would I dive again into ambient refulgence; try to prove there once was a paradise of amber, second in splendor only to the sun?

In advance of a scalding wall of ash, glass softened, the harbors boiled; or water rose through and then above the bogland. In any case, the continent was clean gone.

Relieved at familiar disappointment, I go under, susceptible to nitrogen narcosis, sure to be thoughtless and grand among the fry of invention. A sunken island west of the end of the known world.

Urchins plead from a kelp holdfast; drifters pump and trail. Below this depth, pressure replaces bones and muscle; direction is lost. I only want to help the fish breathe.

The stream's run dry above Devil's Gate Dam and the sycamores have finished for the year, lost early in the fast shadows of the canyon. I refuse to remember your kiss, and so have remembered it.

Pale nasturtium leaves tremble, shake a few silver drops in their pans as if there is a moment, as if what might have been isn't as heavy as the whole sky.

I count to myself as I listen to you speak.

Not you. You.

I am in two houses at once.